T0164944

B.C. Saved Me

PART 1

shaneak

Order this book online at www.trafford.com
or email orders@trafford.com

Most Trafford titles are also available at major online book retailers.

© Copyright 2011 Shaneak.
All rights reserved. No part of this publication may be reproduced, stored in a retrieval
system, or transmitted, in any form or by any means, electronic, mechanical, photocopying,
recording, or otherwise, without the written prior permission of the author.

Printed in the United States of America.

ISBN: 978-1-4269-7486-1 (sc)
ISBN: 978-1-4269-7488-5 (hc)
ISBN: 978-1-4269-7487-8 (e)

Library of Congress Control Number: 2011912347

Trafford rev. 08/11/2011

 www.trafford.com

North America & international
toll-free: 1 888 232 4444 (USA & Canada)
phone: 250 383 6864 ✦ fax: 812 355 4082

Table of Contents

Chapter 1: love

REMEMBRANCE OF LOVE

I saw a dream perched upon a star...
I didn't see you, now I wonder where you are.
If my time comes, promise me you'll move on.
Just understand, and know that I'm gone.
But I live within your heart...
At every beat... at every thump.

Just remember those good times we shared.
Those moments in my life you were once there.
For as my life ahead will never be told
Let me live for today...
Let me be glad for tomorrow...
And promise me that in the end...
You shall feel no sorrow...

Know that our love was well worth having.
And as long as you remember it, it will be everlasting.
One breath... One beat...
As we slowly take the days on...
Banking every memory.

SPILLED OUT FROM PROTECTION

I am wish-wash like the water that pulls the sand back into the sea.
I am burdened like a mother who gives birth to an unwanted seed.
I love but love does not love me.
So I reach out to thee.

I called upon a revolution to end the torment that lies in my heart.
I fought a civil war; lied to the retrograde and hid from the police.
I am in search of salvation and your heart is what I seek.
Will you show me the way?

I'm searching to find a way home…
A safer place to roam.
I am dignified, however, denied my right to be.
So I'm looking for something; for no one will allow me to be me.
Tell me… What do you see?

Can I cry a different cry?
A lonely cry.
For I don't cry a painful cry because you can't hurt me.
Your words… your touch…
Nothing.
For I cannot feel pain.
Yet my emotions leak out like a floodplain.

Spilling out from Protection

THE ONLY ONE

Can a heart be so strong, yet so weak.
I am feeble.
My soul I give to thee, to love…
Cherish for eternity.
I am bound to another by his love.
But tis not he that I place on high, it is u that I place above.
All that may enter my heart, but you have taken my soul.

I run and hide for others may come.
And pray that one day, you shall be the only one.
To love…
Cherish me, Hold me near.

I weep to have you,
Dream about you.
Shiver when I need you.
And will always love you.

You are the salt in my tears.
My light through my fears.
My nectar of honey.
The green in my money.
And the brightness of my sun.
You are… the one… I love…
The only one.

If I must run and hide and await your call,
Rather than stand appalled…
I shall wait under the nearest rock,
Stand under the closest waterfall.
For you are the one I love…
The only one.

Circumstance may place our lives on hold.
As we experience our lives separately.
Stories untold…
I shall wait until you come.
For our work apart will then be done.
And you and I shall live in harmony,
Love each other for eternity.
I you and you me.

To Love…
For you are the one I love…

I am the one you love
For I U and U me.
The one and only one.

DROWNING HEARTS

Let me drown in an ocean full of ♥'s.
Let them surround my body and pull me
under....
Making way for their different types of
affection...
Emotions shaped and designed to its own
perfection.

Showing me hate in all forces that it can
come...
Placing me on its list at number one...
Show me love to the highest degree...
And love me unconditionally...
Show me tears...that would flood the
ocean...
As I drown drinking its potions....
Show me joy through all the madness....
As another presents me with sadness....

Let me drown in an ocean full of ♥'s...
Let me soak in its essence...
As I spill out in confession
As if I was at the alter...
Praying for repentance of my sins...
As I drink in the potion of my drowning ♥'s

I see the different types of healing...
I see the different types of feeling...
I see what many aren't sharing...
I see what was presented as daring...
Flashing before my eyes... I see death...
Yet hear the cries of hearts bleeding
Feeding off one another....
As they drown in sorrow...
Forgetting about tomorrow...

And I sink... deeper into the ocean....
lungs filled with their potion...
I sink.... Looking up at those who stayed
behind...
Those who wanted to give it one more try...
And I hold onto those that gave themselves
to me...
Those who allowed me to feed...
As I sink to the bottom of the ocean…

I LOVE YOU

My heart spills over like the glass that now
lies on the floor.
I love you like the wind that reaches out to
the four corners of the world
I dream of you dancing, running into my
arms on a cold winter night.
I can feel you trying to keep me warm
needing my body to generate heat.
The love that reaches down into the depths
of your soul.

I miss your love.
For like a rose I will die without the light of
you in my life.
Without the water that you give me to
quench the love I have for you.
For like a rose In need of its resources,
I'm in need of natural forces;
Those things that keep the love going,
the flower growing.
Just a sprinkle of your time to make
sure I'm still alive

Still alive in your soul, in your heart is
where I wish to reside.
Cherish you, need you,
want and love you for eternity.
Time spent, placed at a cost,
for if spent unwisely will surely be lost.
I say again, I love you, I can tell you that I
truly do.

What is my world if you do not reside there?
What is my life if you do not exist in it?
What... Who… Where would I be without
you?
Could you find me?
Save me from that wretched life I
would live without you.
Sweet love... my dear sweet love.
I truly do love you, I need you, I want you, I
adore you.
With all thoughts, with all dreams in my
world, in your world.
To place in an existence called reality.

VALENTINES

What does it mean?
Love scenes and empty dreams...
Dozen roses and Luxurious Panty Hoses...
V for Vital...
A for Always
L for Love
E for Eternity
N for No
T for Time
I for I
N for Now
E for Everlasting...
Miss interpretation of words...
Heard through centuries of Gossip...
Dropped it...
And will no longer celebrate the Holiday...
Love always...Anytime, Anywhere.
Emotions will always flow...

WAITING ON LOVE

I dream of love like so many do.
But will that dream someday come true.
They say it will come when its time.
But time waits for no one.
And what may work for others, may not work for some.
I dream of a mans touch almost every day.
Expressing how we feel in every way.
No problems should occur; No reason for me to complain.
But I'm sure every woman at least once dreamed the same.

I just wish to love.
But I will continue to dream, waiting on the stars above.

ETERNITY

Your sweet nectar of love fondles with my tongue.
As I graciously put my arms around you.
Holding on to you like the last beat of my heart.
Your enchanting smile looks down upon me.
A sweet sensation of joy overcomes me.
Love floats all around us... Even within us.
And I stare...
At you while my heart beats faster and faster with every second.
I could tell you I love you ten times over.
Within you I am lost.
Within me I give thee all of me... Not willing to leave any of me behind.
For now until ETERNITY; I am yours and you are mine.

HERE

Here is my heart and soul.
'Tis this is what I give to you.
To take care and tightly hold
Never let go and always be true
Here is my body and mind.
To you I give my all
Within me love is what you'll find.

A LOVE LIKE YOURS

A Love like yours is so Brand New.
And all I can say is "I love you."
You fill me up with so much joy.
I feel like a child with a brand new toy.
I want to touch it and play with it too.
But more than anything, I want to tell you, "I love you."
Your sweet words of gently song,
They console me as I lay in your arms.
Do I have any doubt in my mind about you?
No, this is why I can say, "I love you."
A love like yours is all I need.
A love like yours in only for me.

Chapter 2: Relationships

IMPERFECTION/PERFECTION

I detected a wrinkle…
All fine lines gone…
I saw a bump…
A pimple now shown.
But I love me regardless of the color of my eyes.
Say you love me…
Even with my ugly cries.
I just washed my hair.
And it's really nappy.
I had a bad day at work…
And at home I'm feeling sappy.
Will you comb my hair?
Even if it's hard to comb through
Will you cheer me up?
Take away my color blue.
I'm not perfect…
Not looking for imperfection…
Only just to love you…
And surely some affection.
You know I'm getting fat and I have to buy a whole new size.
I don't feel like cooking tonight and I hope you're not wondering why?
I got a callous on my foot today…
From wearing those heels…
Would you sand it away…
It's starting to peel.
I love you unconditionally as if I loved myself.
I love you regardless of your imperfection for I love no one else.
You know…I sometimes snore in my sleep.
And have a tendency to whine.
And even though I may look bad in the morning
Will you still tell me I'm fine.
My perfection lies in the love that I have for you…
That we share together through and through
And regardless of my imperfection…
Regardless of your imperfection…
As we grow and love each other with so much affection.
The love we share is to the highest perfection
That anyone could ever know!!!

I FOUND ME

I found me lost…
Undefined in time, indulged in the way you were.
Wanting and needing you.
You gave me love.

I found that time meant nothing when it came to you.
That forever was us and never did not exist.
And in the mist when the dew cleared away
When the love shall fade away.
I found me lost within you.
I fell in love with you.
And to say who you are.
A man, not mine, undefined.
In time, I pray would be mine.
But to wait, I dare to say
To play myself as a fool
I shall not want you.
Yet I found me missing you.
Wanting and needing you.
Feeling you deep inside of me.
Not just physically but mentally.
Mind, body and soul.
As we become one making our halves whole.
Can I do this?
I dare not say.
I pray the lord will give me strength to walk away.
Then I found me
Crying because of the position
I have placed myself in.
How can I begin to understand?
And place on demand my feelings.
Not to care of another feelings.
So there I found me.
Lost

HOW CAN I WALK AWAY

How can I walk away from
all that I dreamed?
How can I walk away from you and me?
How can I walk away and never look back?
How can I walk away without
knowing all the facts?
How can I walk away not knowing
if you cared?
How can I walk away wondering if you
would've been their?
How can I walk away without
giving it a try?
How can I walk away without
saying good-bye?
How can I walk away without
telling you I love you?
How can I walk away knowing that
never again...
      will I be with you.

HOW I MISS U MUCH

Your smile is of an innocent child.
Your lips so tender to the touch.
And of those thoughts...How I miss you
much?

Your body is so hard, firm, and sleek.
Thinking of you everyday,
you stay on my mind for weeks.
And of those thoughts, How I miss you
much?

The funny jokes you tell.
Or simply the way you smell.
The Softness of your voice,
I couldn't resist you even if I had a choice
And of those thoughts, How I miss
you much?

Your respectful and sweet.
One of the nicest men I could meet.
And of those thoughts, How I miss you
much?

HE DID NOT FEEL THE SAME

He was the man I truly adored

But he did not feel the same.

A man I would love forever more.
But he did not feel the same.

To him anything I would give.
But he did not feel the same.

And in his world I wanted to live.
But he did not feel the same.

I treasured his sweet enduring smile.
But he did not feel the same.

Just to be next to him I'd travel a thousand miles.
But he did not feel the same.

He's everything in a man I dream him to be.
But he did not feel the same.

I only wish that he loved me.
But he did not feel the same.

Instead he left me used and abused.
Lost in him, …dazed and confused.
Full of things I didn't understand.
Only knowing that I wanted him for my man.
But he did not feel the same.

Loving a man until your heart is content.
Then today came and yesterday he went.
And still, not once…. Did he feel the same.

WITHSTAND THE RAIN

The sudden distant cry, I wonder why…
I hear my voice, without a choice…
Calling your name.
Can I withstand the rain?

In time, I wonder if you'll be all mine.
For each other we shall take care.
And together we shall share…
Our love.
But can I withstand the rain.

I sit on a curb…
Silence…
With no words.
Waiting…
Wanting you to come and get me.
But you are nowhere to be found.
You left me lost, Downtown…
I'm trying to withstand the rain.

When you leave me at home alone.
And for hours you are gone.
No info as of where, As if I didn't care.
My heart still aches.
And I cry out, begging you to take it away.
I want to withstand the rain.

Our communication is so good.
And well, as one we are understood.
We love each other unconditionally.
We stimulate each other mentally.
I would detest another who would hurt your heart.
I would die if were to ever be torn apart.
But can I withstand the rain.

Should I say yes when I want to say no?
Should I say stay when I want you to go?
Will you understand when I beg you not leave?
Will you always in me believe?
That I will be true, always love you.
For better or worse, take care of you.

Withstand the Rain

LOVE CHANGE - Part I

I brought you love of whispering
secrets...
My darkness turned to daylight...
as the moon beam down upon my
window pane..
Laid with dew from a misty afternoon..
Bringing forth a beautiful morning.

You gave me love as the sunset rises
above snowy mountains...and the rain
settles upon
a teary face and an empty soul.
You took me into your heart, your
soul, your mind.
You gave it to me so willingly and like
a child.
I took it grabbed hold and promised to
never let go.

I loved you for I knew nothing else to
do but love you.
To nurture you and make you mine...
To love and hold till the end of time...

Now I'm lost...mixed with emotions....
like lotions...being rubbed
in my skin...I don't know how to begin
the change.

LOVE CHANGE - Part II

So now we go through the phases...
the mazes....
that get us lost in a realm of
sometimes darkness...
let me be strong and see the light.

Let me still love you regardless of the
fright...
that I have from the changes we've
made...

What is different?
What is the same?
And yet devotedly yours.... I still
remain....
Chained to your love...
to you...

I should have known that the tides
would soon rise...
I should have known that the skies
would turn gray...
And without dismay...
I will not turn away....
But continue to love you....

For I know that the waves will go back
out to see...
and you will still be with me....
I know that the skies will again be
clear....
and I will be right here....
Through our love change....

I ENGAGED IN A LOVE AFFAIR

I have engaged in a love affair.
and to love I dared…
I pulled my heart out from within my soul.
I have made him part of me, no longer whole

I engaged in a love affair.
From beginning to end.
And I can't even fathom, no I can't even begin.
To think what it would be like alone.
Once he is gone.

I engaged in a love affair.
A love like no other.
We shared everything, from one to another.
Our hugs were everlasting, kisses with such passion
progress was old fashion
and yet it isn't lasting.

I engaged in a love affair.
That abruptly came to an end
He wants to know if we can still be friends.
Even though the fire still burned and the love continued to grow
He cried about not being man enough and in return he had to go.

To let me love him just to leave
And all the stories he told, all the dreams
In him I believed.
But he's leaving me because he feels he's not man enough for me.

CALLING YOU - PART 1 (THE CALL)

Lying on my bed thinking of last night.
I want to call but then come a hesitation.
A tense fixation.
Thinking of what I would say.
So I decide not to call today but dial the number anyway.

Listening as the phone rings
Waiting with anticipation.
A face shown with aggravation.
Theirs no answer.
So then I push the dial tone.
Cause he's not even home.

CALLING YOU - PART 2 (THE FALLEN)

I sat by the phone today waiting for you to call.
The phone never rung and my heart began to fall.
I went out today I was suppose to meet you at the mall.
You never showed, my heart began to fall.
So I pick up the phone and decide to give you a call.
You weren't even home, my heart begins to fall.

I waited time and time again.
And how many times I've tried with you I can't even begin.
Now I've finally given up.
No more waiting
No more trying
My heart has now dropped.

He wrote me a song…
Written from deep within…
His soul….
He said it was me he loved…
And he wished to have me to hold…
I read his words written down on paper…
More like music to my ears…
It showed his undying love for me…
It showed his fears…
And with that…I shed tears….
The sounds that came from these words…
Just on this flat piece of paper….
It was like a razor tearing into my soul….
And at that point…all I wanted was him to hold…
His words…written down on paper…
Sung me a lullaby…with the background sound
Of a woodpecker pecking on a piece of wood…
It told me of the frog who needed a princess to turn him back into Robin Hood.
His words…written down on paper…
And I cried…for his love was there…
And I question my love…I questioned if I care…
About these words…written down on paper…
Yet their letters jumped at me…
Relaxed me…
Reassured me…
That he would be there….
They sung me to sleep at night…
When there was no one to hold…
They kept me warm during the winter cold…
These words written down… on his paper.
And in harmony…Each mellow tone, shown in every verse…
I've read so many times…you would have thought I had rehearse…
the lines…every single one…
Every single time…I read…
His words…written on paper.

GOT ME THINKING

You got me thinking about what I use to do.
You got me questioning me and you.
Makes me wonder how strong you are.
Makes me wonder if we'll get that far.

You got me thinking about right and wrong.
You got me questioning just how long…
We're going to last.
Will we come to past and be just a memory.
And eventually,
We will have new and different lives.
Oh how I strive to see the light.
Now that you've got me thinking.

Thinking about my morals and all of my values.
Let me practice integrity because I don't believe in infidelity.
Yet I'm not practicing what I preach and on to you I leech.
Are you beginning to follow me?

You are man…
Internal within my mind…
Is where you will find...
          You.
In such a divine manner.
I want to be the answer.
To all your dreams, wishes and prayers.
But I dare to ask that of you.
I hope you're starting to follow me.

You see…
I get a tingly sensation when hit with an ejection of your love.
You are divinely, sublimely…
Construed within my mental.
Using a stencil to dig and pry you out of my soul.
Yet I can't control the urge to love you.
Have you caught up yet?
While you got me thinking.

PASSED ME BY

I got a date tonight.
Maybe he's Mr. Right.
But is that what I'm looking for?
Do I want more?

I passed him on the street the other day.
And he kindly said, "Hello Miss lady."
I greeted him with a smile.
Then gave him my number to call after while.

He called last night.
We talked till the morning light.
So sweet were the words that came out of his mouth.
Indefinitely sweet, I truly doubt.

Now we've been talking for about two months.
And yes, he's a good man. I ain't even gonna front.
But once again, is that truly what I want.

He treats me like royalty.
A man that knows how to define loyalty.
Never lets me down, always be around.
He told me he loved me for the first time.
Now I see the sign.
Its time for me to go.
Why? I don't' even know.

I know he'll treat me well.
Unfortunately, in love with him I have not fell.
For him I had no feelings.
And to me what we had, had no meaning.

He's a good man though.
Yet I still want to let him go.
Now he sees there is nothing their.
And from that he tells me farewell.

Six months down the line.
After all that time.
I wonder why
I let that man pass me by.

Chapter 3: Experience

FIND ME

You'll find me wrapped up in weeds.
My heart lying in my hand as it slowly bleeds…
Tears in my eyes,
Not yet fallen…But you're waiting on me to cry.

You'll find me lost in him
From beginning to end.
Unable to find a way out.
Yet he does not hear me when I scream and shout
Out his name in a cry for love…
The purity like the whiteness of a dove.

You'll find me caged within my heart.
Like a prisoner in a jail cell.
Searching for a psychic my future I pray she would tell.
If I should die a lonely soul.
Or always have you to hold.

You'll find me blown to the fours seas.
Down upon my knees, begging the lord to bless me
My sins that I have made; may they be forgiven as I pray.

Or just find me…
Search out for me
Seek and you shall find
That in time.
My soul once whole
Now empty and shallow.
Find me too soon or too late.
Which ever comes first… Shall tell my fate.

CONTROL THE THOUGHTS

My days numbered.
Stop!!!
I can hear the thunder.
The rumble in my heart
And that streak of lightning that tore it apart

Thoughts spill in my mind
Creating dreams that I find
To be nightmares
No I dare…
Not tell their stories
Forgotten like bad memories.
The screams that I constantly hear.
Is it within me that I fear.
Hiding behind the life that I choose to live.
Losing myself in a rage, only to engage
In the sinful acts of love.
If only amnesia would take control
As I so willing let God take my soul

Should I run or stand still
Thoughts digging in my mind like an electric drill
Only to find a poisoned brain.
On the verge of going insane.
My heart starts beating faster,
As I submit to my thoughts like they were my master.

MY POSITION

What is my position?
At what angle am I looking at my life?
When will I put down the pipe?
When will I want to be a wife?

My position…
Set at a different angle, squares, circles and triangles.
I dangle from a string, not interested in wearing rings.
I am subtle, yet wide eyed.
What is my position?

I am searching for a higher learning with greater earnings.
A peaceful life with a man I can call my own.
A place I can call home. I want to go to Fife.
The great land of Switzerland.
I want to stay in Italy, travel to Rome.

What is my position?
When I no longer make friends but associates.
When I distance myself from those who love me?
I have classified myself as nonexistent.
Yet I am reminiscent of the days, the way things use to be.
Memories…

What is my position?
How must I transition?
Shape me, map myself out on paper.
Drape me with the cloth of insanity.
For I am demanding to know my position.

I haven't got a clue of where I am.
Let alone worrying about where I want to be!!!!
Let me do me!!!
For I need to reconstruct my identity.
Find out what really makes me happy.

What is my position?
When the dark clouds come and go and I keep praying for snow.
Except I live in the south, and unless God is making plans…
The white side don't come to the south side.
So I'm looking to go North, be it west or east.
But they say for a country girl like me, City boys would feast.

I'm not looking to be blind, To me I feel wise...
Enough to get my own.
Since seventeen, that's four years I've been grown.

So what in this world is my position?!!
I don't have intentions on being classified as part of this society.
For I feel the government is citizen robbery.
I have no intentions on being a statistic of any classification.
But there is a class for every part of the proclamation.

I have plans to move forward, but what of my destination.
I've been doing so much procrastination.
Yet I'm about to lead the Chariot Home.
Still, I'm not sure of **My Position.**

RUN AWAY

I'm a runaway child
lost in the child...
forced into the wild...
made to reconcile..
with my own differences...
my shoulda...
coulda
woulda
wanna
hadta
wish I could
hope I don't...
cause I can't
not sure how...
someday will
be what I have always dreamed to be...
look past my use to beeeeessss......
I'm a lost in a valley so low I can't climb out...
so I shout out for a hand...
if not your hand then GODs hand....
to lift me up
take me away....
and I pray... I cry... I dream... I scream... I fight... I shout... I whine...
I pray... I pray... I pray... I pray....
that one day...
all my past hurts... all my past hurts...
my bad dreams.... all my bad dreams...
all my misfortunes...
my sins.... all my sins....
all my disappoints...
my hate.... all my hate....
will soon fade away.
The sudden dark cloud that falls down upon me...
when my sun is shining so bright...
I want to see no more...
I want to go no more...
to that place...
in my head... in my head... in my head.... in my head....
where I wished I was dead...
I was dead...

I want to go no more.
Take me to that place...
where I know I am sure...
where I am sure... I'm sure...
that ...all will be forgiven....
Good-bye to the bad...
good riddens...
I wish to be free... I wish to be free...
I dream to be free.
I want to be free... I want to be free!!!
I ran away...from all my brutality...
but yet it is still stored within my mentality....
it has clouded my train of thought...
kept me from opening up my heart....
I wish to be free...
I'm a runaway child...
running from me....

TO FEAR KNOWLEDGE OF THYSELF

My stomach is in a knot.
I can feel the fire burning.
As my stomach boils, my soul slowly removes itself.
Away from the texture, the cover that keeps my insides in.
That keeps my blood flowing through.

How long will it beat?
How long will it hurt?
If I'm not happy then who am i?
If I am not free, then what am I suppose to be?

Can I love?
Can I hate?
Should I feel and never take?
To understand what wonders that my life may hold.
Or watch every day, unknowingly as it unfolds.

I hide but surely not from what I will soon be.
Let me go and become in peace with me.
Another world, immortality.
Let me hide behind my dreams.
Let me live behind what seems like peace to me.

Let me go, I can't cry forever..
I can't shed no tears, not even over my fears.
Pain consistently drowns me in misery.
Constantly pounding on me.
I got to reach for something.
If not I would obtain nothing.
Just to hide the emotions within.
Bleeding inside due to a lost destiny; due to corruption of sin.
Can't fight it no more.
Can't hide it no more.
Uncertain of what to do.
But I must learn and understand the real truth.

MYSTY EYED BROWN NOSE GIRL

Don't you dare shy away from me.
Let your eyes shine bright as the clear blue sea.

The tears that start to cover you pupil.
Don't let them fall.
Become frugal.

The pain that has pierced your heart.
All laid upon, stomped on and torn apart.
Laden and lost… dreams sold at a cost.

Tell me dear child who has hurt your heart.
Did you fall and sprang your knee?
Did someone hold you down;
Told you could not go to the bathroom to pee.

My poor mysty eyed brown nose girl.
Let me shower you with diamonds and pearls.
Let me take you for the world you must see.
Help you stand tall and believe in thee.

Yet still you hang your head.
Saying prayers, wishing you were dead.
Have the rays from the sun turn your soul sullen?
Have you run from the world like a convicted felon?

Hiding yourself for all not to see.
Denying yourself what belongs to thee.
Reaching out for someone to take away the pain.
And in return love you did not gain.

My poor mysty eyed brown nose girl.
Let me give you the world.
Make your dreams a reality.
As your eyes shine bright as the shining sea.

MY PEN HAS NO INK

I can't write my pen has no ink.
The flow just won't come out of me.
I got so much deep down inside.
But my pen just won't let it glide…
Across that paper.

I'm like a bin and all my trash is within.
I've tried writing it on paper.
But it just won't in my favor.
I've tried putting it up on the screen.
But the cursor just sits there as I continue to dream.
About what is running through my mind.
How can I find the answer to all my mysteries?
How can I find me?

I can't write my pen has no ink.
The flow just won't come out of me.
I'm searching for a resolution attached to the conclusions.
That I have distorted, retorted back and forth in my mind.
I just can't find the answer to all my mysteries.
I just can't find me.

I've been looking at this pen for weeks.
And my thoughts refuse to come out of me.
I just wish they would spill themselves on paper.
Then disappear like vapor.

I need to release the tension that I have within.
I need to fly away like the Raven.
Even the smallest birdie, but it just won't come out of me.
I've been shaking it.
Considered breaking it.
My soul is screaming inside, "PLEASE LET THESE THOUGHTS OUT!"
But my pen refuses to write what it's all about.

I can't write my pen has no ink.
The flow just won't come out of me.

BEGINNING OF THE END

He took from me what I would have cherished the most.
A host, now ghost.
In my memory...
Once a sensory of motherhood.
Gone back to the norm.
A form of worship that I would have honored for the rest of my days.
Now I lay, wondering why I had to pay.
My first never truly my first.
Nothing I can call my own.
Grown and deep down inside I feel even more alone.

A foolish child.
For a smart one would have realized.
Anguish in the soul.
An emptiness that will always stick to the heart.
Unleashed, released... truthfully.
Yet still I deny me.
What is truly mine rightfully.

Can't go back.
Surely can't change the pain.
Gained by my own selfish dreams.
Accrued by my own selfish means.
Seems, that doors close and often you do have options.
But only one when it's all done.
A choice, reckoned by your own voice
Embedded within your own conscious.
Uncertain of how cautious to be.
You can't laugh and you can't call it fun.
Just another experience that you drill in your head as a lesson.
To recognize the reason and what it cost.
To see victory even when it was lost.
For some things just wasn't me to be.
Even though you thought that it was suppose to be.

MY DEAR FATHER

As I stand extended over Niagara Falls, and out your name I call.
Lord my Father.
Transcendent over life in time, say you're mine.
As I share you with everyone.
Glorify me.
Please don't deny me.
Your love

So while my mind wonders
It ponders on the life that you have given me.
Thankfully.
I am mentally holding onto my sanity.
I dream of fruit fly and butterfly, catching dandelions as I cry.
You whisper words of endearment in my head.
I fear enchantment of the heavens.
A creator whom has seeded the barren forest.
The angels as one sing a gospel chorus.
Your word rings in my ear. Hymn from Psalms chapter 3.

Thank you Father.
For you have cleansed my soul.
Then sitting under the midnight moon, perched upon a sand dune.
I dig deep into the heavens earth, asking of my worth.
Can I be worthy of you?
An immortal that will always be true.
I love you my dear Father.

Guiding me to a victory I have not yet won.
Teaching me things I have not yet learn.
Allowing me to understand what I have not yet done.
I see a red sky under a green sea.
I see the whale flying in the sky as the eagle swims by.
Watching me be all that I can be.
I float to the surface and fly to the top.
I dip into the blue green sea.
I shed tears with the urge to flee.
Out from the sympathy of my sinful endeavors.
Much to me being clever.
I have hidden my soul from the world.
I have taken control of my life since I was a little girl.

Now I give it to you.

For I love you.
My Dear Father.

LET YOU IN MY WORLD

Let me tell you of a day old dream.
Stitched at the seams.
Fine lines
Undefined
By the patches of a bright colored quilt.

I sing the song of pain…
My body is mentally drained.
Guided into the thickening of the forest.
In the distance I hear a chorus…
Singing my sad songs…
Where do I belong?

Am I seen, yet not heard.
Are my words like ridicule…?
Simply an annoying verse.
That I just rehearse
To be ignored.

My triumphant plea…
For sensibility…
I'm a stranger in the late night.
Seeking to do right…
For wrong is not in my vocabulary,
But on the contrary.
Can you see what I see?

To feel and know it's real.
To cry and know why.
To comprehend and understand.
To love and never to hate
To dream, dreams into reality as if it was fate.
Let me let you into my World.

Chapter 4: Our Society/ Government

OUR SOCIETY

The government base things on statistics; let us be realistic.
Do they truly see what we see?
Our research is being burned, just like all the other burnings.
Our true identity is being hidden, ridden of all the vile,
That has been infested in our brains.
We have our forefathers and future fathers, many who stand in shame.
In pain from the burdens born on their back.
We lack… a vision.

Yet it burns like an incision being performed on our brain.
We say things are still the same.
Still a color… turning our backs on our brothers.
No love or respect for one another.
From the streets to the suburbs, to the cigarettes and natural herbs.

We are just another statistic in our own society.
We yell out high way robbery.
Cause the police just got off, for knocking off
another brother, could've been our mother.
But that's just our society.

We watch TV shows, videos and movies about facilities.
That hold our brothers hostage for selling to make a living.
Due to the statistics that has been placed on them do to our society.
Molesters go free, after doing a year, maybe two or three..
What about me, the children, the mothers.
The babies, gone crazy from drugs being pumped into their blood stream.
From drug addicted mothers during pregnancy.
When will we wake up to reality.
To know that suburbs do not eliminate herbs.
And who said that if they built a fence, no one can get in.
We are a society living in a government
that's using us, abusing us.

How can I get in the political bracket.
Congressman can I be your do girl.
Clint let me get down on my knees.
Free up my creditability.
Like you do for the others, before they leave.

How can I be set aside from the other.
Try and look pass my color.
If it wore a neck tie and ate turkey on rye

Will that keep me from being an outcast?
In the days past will I still be neglected, for one has projected.
That if we became more civilized, people would realize.
 That we are people in this society.

I feel segregation every time I walk into a room.
The first thing many assume is my color.
Initially I'm a sister, then seek to understand my mentality.
Sit and talk to me, get to know me.
Yet we still live in a society where we still want 40 acres and mule.
Which is cool.
I can get rich, off the land.
Sell it back to the man.
Cause I know he'll be the highest bidder.
But what about my brothers and sisters.
Still watching TV, reconstructing their mentality.
With all its lies and over indulgence in the happening of the day.
We pray for a better place.
Did we forget that this world is what we created?
People as a whole.
Now we've gone holy, soley because of our wrong.
But if we were strong in Gods word in the beginning.
Would we still have to worry when this world will be ending.

This is our society.
Personally this whole thing is high way robbery.
Struggling to survive, thousands trying to get by
Everyone is trying to get a piece of the pie.
Want to know how I can get rich quick.
I am so sick of being a part of a society.
Another statistic
They give us a number and keep us in slumber.
To the facts behind those stats.
They can't even see what the average Joe see,
In this big on world that holds a part of our society.

WELFARE AT A STAND!!!

I had a dream....
But it wasn't of welfare...
I had dream...
To be all that I can be...

But I didn't know where to go...
So I just stuck with what I know...
I got a job but it didn't pay my bills
So I moved back home with my moms...
just decided to chill...

I had dream...
But it wasn't of welfare...
I had dream...
Just wasn't sure what I wanted to be...

So I worked...at the Mc D's...
Flipping burgers...
Asking if they wanted cheese....
Met a man that said he would be good to me...
Until he loaded me up with his seed....
Then decided he had a dream...
and just like that he up and leaves.

I had a dream....
But it wasn't of welfare...
I had dream...
But now I got a family....

My mom can't take the noise...
I decide I'm not dating anymore boys...
Realized I got to get out on my own....
I know social services will help me get a home...
Just need a decent job to keep it....
And hell some low rent and extra spending...
In a sense I feel like I'm winning...

So I'm content is what you think...
That so low I sink...
That I'm just on welfare...
But I had a dream....
And it wasn't about being on welfare...
I had a dream...
Just wasn't sure what I wanted to be...
But I had a dream....
And it wasn't about being on welfare...
I had a dream....
But now I got a family.

NOW WHAT SHALL WE BE?

Sleepy eyes, don't you cry.
Dry those tears away.
Wipe the rain from your face.
For the sun will bring a better day.
Hidden words and discovered poems,
As we walk the life of an Omen.
Time shared and time past; we are the everlasting,
as we continuing basking.
In the rays of our sunlight, much to our delight.
We shall find a rhyme that speaks of the wonders of our own world within us.
Finding peace through the retrograde, death will soon fade
We pray for the souls that are lost, given at a cost.
But remember with a memory that carries the name on.
Shall we sing the same song?
Domineering and pain inflicted.
Lives depicted, people evicted, children restricted.
By the rules of the world today.
Let us pray for our souls.
We sin, drink gin, eat fish fin and always want to win.
Souls blown in the wind, running out of time.
Measured on a clock, tick tock.
Wondering when will yours stop.
Hanging by a piece of thread.
Babies that don't get fed end up dead.
And we pay to go to pre-med.
Make college loans, quit school and go back home.
Now in debt to the G-O-V, home based in DC.
Hiring us to fight for a country.
That defies our freedom, by rules and regulations.
We should feel honored for desegregation.
We must prepare for inflation.
A new president up holds the throne.
A country once glorified soon to be gone.
And we stand with what… nothing.
For we stand alone and if we can't stand together.
Whether black , white, sister or brother.
Our empire shall fall.
From the opinions of a single division.
Like an incision, into the souls of many.
Money, we shall no longer have plenty.
But dimes and cents, braking in half the peppermints.
Must we decrease our percentage?

Must we constantly speak while no one hears our verbiage.
For us to stand together, "Birds of a feather flock together"
We run where theirs warmer weather.
But who will stay and withstand the cold.
To take care of the sick and the old.
Our country brought into poverty had sovereignty.
Now what shall we be?

IN THIS WORLD

Step out!
Away from the visual eye
Take a deep sigh and then you start to cry
For the pain you have been through all these years
Quickly come the flowing tears
Drip...Drop.
When will they stop?
How much pain can one endure?
As much as a baby born pure.
 Looking out to a world lost...
And you can't see that through your pain
You're hurting me.
An ashy face from salt water.
Pay attention to your child, Son or daughter

Ignoring the biggest factors.
Whether you know it or not, it does matter.
A head hung low a smile not shown.
Will they remember you?
Were you well known?
Yet even one who is the most mystique.
Once gone someone will see.

The questions that we constantly ask about our future
Solve the past be it your heart, mind or soul
To move on one must take control
One must find what life means to them
Taking precautions and stepping out on a limb.
Undignified, Mystified, Truly obliged by their successful goals
Some lucky
Others, their life they took control.
Guide me
Hide me
Ride me off into the sunset.
Take me away from a life where people always expect
Something, if not nothing
Yet wondering, when they are going to do something for nothing.

I encourage, No longer discourage
Yet allow people to believe
In themselves so that they may achieve

Their own dreams
Like everyone else who has or shall succeed
In this world that I, You and me live in.
Created pure, built in sin.
I don't recommend that one should follow
Those worldly values
But we all will pay our dues
Young, old... The brand new.

A destiny set
Untold to you.

DISCRIMINATION

I am cripple, my left foot toes have tripled.
If I wear sandals, promise you won't stare me down.
Promise you won't frown.
I can still walk and talk better than you.
Why can't you just help me to my destination, instead of staring like a fool?

I am Cuban and I don't speak English.
Must I be punished because I can't say a complete sentence?
You don't know my background and you don't know who I am.
Just give me time, I need time to learn.
Why can't you be nice enough to teach me some of the words?

I am black, rich in color.
Why are you afraid of me?
I work and live just like every human being.
What are you looking at?
Tell me what it is you're really seeing.

I am a man, hear me roar.
And because of my past time, you're intimidated by me more.
Just because of my stance and the way I work out.
I wouldn't hurt you. That's not what I'm about.

I am woman, gentle to the soul.
What is it about me you like to control?
You take my femininity for a weakness.
You put me down when I'm at my best.
Who's to say I can't be just like you?
Who's to say I can't do what you do?
Except you.

Yes I am, Homosexual!!!
I'm white, black, Hispanic and Korean.
I'm proud, but you look at me in discuss.
You make a constant fuss about what I do.
What have I done to you?
Who's to say you're not down with it too.
But then again, this isn't about the truth.

I am old, weak and feeble.
Once young like you and you'll be like me one day soon.
But you fuss when I drive slow on the road.

You trample over me when I'm crossing the street.
I'm suppose to be your elder but you don't respect me.

I am young and I am free!!!
I am simply what you use to be.
You judge me by your past decisions
But unlike you my life is different.
So why can't I have my say.
Just like you did back in the day.

DISCRIMINATION LEAVES A DIVIDED NATION

GOVERNMENT YEAR 2001

Come on my people, talk to me.
Obviously we are feeble and weak.
Oblivious to the Governments Plan.
You may think this is all about the white and black man.
We must step behind the color
We are being used as human beings.
As we continue to feen off of all objects that don't mean a thing.
This is about the RICH VS. POOR
Either you're in our out, soon the underpaid will shout!
"TAX BREAK!!"
How much will the Government take!!!
All those people that got laid off.
Thinking you're straight cause the governments paying you off.
Refund money comes up short.
Double take on Tax Reports..
Where was your tax deductible.
See its far from a white and black issue.
We're in a recession based on our governments misuse.
Of our Glorious Funds.
And our President still has a voting rate above 81, "Percent that is"
Stock has not rise and the homeless are still outside
Yet we give millions to feed another country.
This is not funny.

Our strong proud men and women out to the rescue.
We close our eyes to the real truth.
A battle based upon an opinion.
The lost was over a thousand.
Now out for justice, we go and make a ruckus.
While our country continues to bleed
Other countries feed off of our impurities.
Tradition gone with identity.
Values lost in our own beliefs.
We pray for peace, but don't have the patience for guidance.
When will we learn the spirituality of our Country.
It cries and whimpers from the pain.
Its being drained.
Not just the Earth but at the birth of our children.
They feed off of you and me.

Some where we got lost, crossed between right and wrong.
Handshakes and Legal Documents.
Proclamations and Amendments
For each of our souls, the earth makes us whole.
We were taught peace within before our first breath began.
We must reach into our spirituality to find peace.
That's what makes us whole, that what makes us us.
Before we existed, our Forefathers existed.

MY KING TURNED ME INTO A CRACK QUEEN!!!

I loved you.
Stood beside you and supported your every decision...
I trusted you with my own life...
Till the day you told me try the white...
I heard it about and knew it was wrong...
But I was sure my baby wouldn't do me no harm...
That first time was really scary...
That angel dust seemed just like the fairies...
I couldn't believe you had me trying that shit...
I'm trying to figure out where the hell you got it...
How long have you been doing it....
What about our kids?

And then we got a pipe and started pulling through the glass...
We me and you...
What we did together...
I'm your children's mother...
Now I'm addicted...
Inflicted...
Pain upon my child...
To see her mommy acting wild...
She caught me in the bathroom...
You talking about leaving soon...
What am I suppose to do...
I know I need help....
But all the pain I felt...
I just need one.... one more hit... and I'll be okay...
I'm sorry baby but your daddy's gone away...
He say he couldn't stay...
But he'll come by and visit you one day...

I'm strong and still drug addicted...
My children and I are about to be evicted...
So I moved to the projects...
I don't stay home anymore...
I need to feed the kids so now I'm a crack whore...
Hope I got enough to get some groceries..
After I buy my eight ball that is...
And what biz...is it of yours?
I heard you were so high the other night you fell down five floors...

The social services came by the other day....
Said they were gonna take the kids away...
Said someone reported me in..
I think it was your cousin...

Isn't like they trying to help...
I know I need some help...
Thanks to my crack king....

Chapter 5: Inspiration

IT'S SO HARD

It's so hard to tell someone no,
When they really need a yes.
Must I confess my differences to a friend
Who just need a friend.

It's so hard to live....
When you struggle every day.
Our life's is a struggle...
Problems we must juggle...
To make us wiser...coming of age.

It's so hard to understand
What we have yet to do.
But one must reconcile...
Empathize on what some go through.
It's so hard to love...
When no one ever loves you back.
Yet how can you not share what many so yearn and need.
Give me love or let me bleed.

It's so hard just to be...
In dreams...
In teams...
In reality.
But what greater accomplishment is their...
Than to succeed from what is hard for you and me....

WAVES OF TRIUMPH

You'll find a wandering tide.
A slow tide with a high rise.
Of water suds that hugs
Your drowning body.
Too weak to get up
Too strong to stay down.
As it pounds into you, taking pieces of you.
Limb by Limb, your focus is to swim.
Until you get to shore, where no more waves can hit thee.
To flee, yet wanting to go back out their eventually.

It is the drive of the high rise that keeps you wanting more.
For when one door closes, another one opens.
Seek and ye shall fine.
A tide of waves, that gaze upon your soul.
As they ride in, sending you under.
Like the thunder, that drives you back to it.
Once again.

READY TO START A NEW DAY

Here I am ready to start a new day.
High horizons seem far away.
Yet I feel as though I can touch it.
I am now feeding off its beauty.
Its energy that brings sunshine graciously.

Finding paths that were once hidden.
Passing obstacles already completed.
What may appear to be finished,
Is just another flower waiting to be bloomed.

Use your mental thought to invest in you.
To appreciate the Divines creation of you.
The Development of your mind.
The wisdom that has came in time.

To give yourself strength to move forward.
To walk through new doorways.
With the WILL to close ones long once passed through.
To step into a meadow of serenity.

The WILL to start a new day!

SOFT SOUNDS

In the midst of all the ruckus.
I scream!!! Yellowing out to the stars.
Come and take thee.
Me…Away from all this noise.

Loudly is the sound of my heart…
Beating quickly…My blood rises
And I so triumphantly try… To disguise…
The Pain.

Let me go where the clouds roam and the stars rest.
And I shall be at my best
With soft sounds surrounding me.

Yet the thunder rumbles across the sky
Lightning strikes…. Threatening my life
What forces could be placed upon the dew?
Where is my soft sounds…I need surrounding me.

Like the ocean tides
Rushing in and dreading to go back out.
Or the silence of the woods…
And the singing of bugs…
Let those soft sounds surround me.

I WANT TO START OVER

I want to start over....
where the green grass grows fast...
and I will come to peace with my past....

I want to start over where I don't know a sole...
Where I am my only hold on life...
And I can sour higher than an eagle...

I have thought of desert land....
Mountains and beach sand....
Swamps and curvy rivers...
I want to go where my soul quivers...
Where I find peace in me...
As I reach out to be all that I can be....
And if I had no self identity in that place I would find me....

I want to start over....
no worries of another...
no past pain....
I will endure the sunshine...
I will withstand the rain...
I want to go 3,000 miles away from home...
A place where I know...no one I know....
Is willing to roam...

I want to be free of all my burdens...
Forget all my hurting...
Those who have hurt me...
Forgive me if I have hurt thee....

I want to start over....
where my past is just a memory....
Thought of but not too fondly....
I just want to put it all behind me...

I have the urge to just up and leave....
To just leave everything...
And go out and live just for me...
But I'm still searching...
I continue urging myself to tread on...
For I know it won't be long,
and soon I will be gone.

To that place where its only me.....
I want to start over....

BATTLE OF THE MIND

I engage in a theory, logic behind my actions.
About to take a step, make a transaction.
I start to wonder with doubt in my mind.
As it begins to evolve, fury is what I find.

I contest the very thought, combat with the brain.
But it continues to grow, a membrane gone insane.
I stumble and shake my head.
My brain decides it wants to fight.
I take a step back and start to concentrate with all my might.

Then it tries to forget all the things I'm trying to do.
I continue to concentrate, telling my brain, "I'm in control of you!!!"
Then my head spins and starts to pound.
I fall to the floor, almost bust my head on the ground.

I shall not go out in defeat.
I only lay there and continue to concentrate.
Struggling to keep the focus as my brain starts to hesitate.
Telling me, "I control this mind."
So I laugh, not trying to start and argument,
For we will know who wins in due time.

I come for combat, if must… war.
For me, you will not destroy.
As we lay there in confusion.
Me and my brain trying to take control.
We simply came to the conclusion.
You are strong and I am too.
Everything you do, I do too.
So let's focus on what's important and work this thing through.

SACRIFICES

A Life is given a chance for love and romance.
For goals and tribulations.
For achievements and pride at graduation.
We often forget that to receive you must give.
That to be happy you must live..
To be fee it must be embedded in you mentality.
But to gain something, to what result could be the fatality.

In an approach to succeed,
How many times must you bleed.
From despair, brain and muscle repair.
Sacrifices at an angle, glanced at but in the distance.
Slowly coming into existence.
As you reach for a better you and with that you shall include.

SACRIFICES

BLOWN IN THE WIND

I am a piece of paper, flimsy and weak.
Easily torn into pieces, no mouth to speak.
I was thrown away, tossed into the trash.
For my days have come to past.

As I loosely release myself from the garbage.
I am caught up on the wind.
Blown across the street, missed by a car.
From the sheet of my thin tail.
Flimsiness of me, helpless as can be.

I search out the corner of a wall, for shelter is what I call… on
Need to secure me from the dangers of the world
Only to find that the economics of such a place leave me dirty and unclean.
Even a little piece of paper like me, dirt should not be seen… on ,
So I continue to go, continue to blow in the wind.

I came across a beach wishing to sail the four seas.
Just the wind and me.
However, I was afraid the wind would leave and I would soak into the sea.
So decided to move on.
Missed by the fire that would burn me to a crisp.
But the heat surely did touch, unfortunately, I did not miss.
And a tip of me, ashes is what it turned. I was badly burned.
The wind cooled me off, told me my time has not come, I'm still young.
As I move with the wind, basking in the sun.
I dream up a place where it is safe… for me.

I SHINE

I stopped to think, to rest my head over by the fountain sink.
I decided to take a drink only to see my reflection.
It shined in the water.
I could have sworn it wasn't mine.
Who would commit such a crime?
To hurt themselves this way.

I rested my head on the bench but every second I would flinch.
I thought it was the breeze but I had on a two shirts and a sweater.
And believe me, they were long sleeve.
So I treaded on, saw a patch of soft green lawn.
I spread my poor body against its grain.
Some guy came running out his house asking me if I had gone insane.
He told to get out of his yard and though it was hard.
I moved on.

See regardless of the misconception, in regards to my perception.
And how others view me.
I kept moving to somewhere safe.
Where I believed and others believed in me.
Confusion set me back, lack of trust had me lost.
Denial kept me hiding the park.
Ducking behind the trees, lying in the weeds.
Now I can stand out for all to see.
Even me!!!

THE STRENGTH IN INSPIRATION

Sweet dreams are made of these all of my fantasies.
Living in reality; yearning for that sweet ecstasy.
Accepting what I cannot change, only what I can rearrange.
Strong is the one that reach for the high.
Weak is the one that does not try.
All you have to do is believe and surely you will achieve.

Never let anyone put you down, always stand your ground.
We're surrounded in a world of jealousy, killed by another's envy.
Forget the strife, forget the pain.
Every body's about what they can gain.
Look out for me and I'll look out for you.
To each other always be true.

The soul may be what carries us on, but it's our mind that makes us strong.
Our body is there for the taking.
A heart made for breaking.
But through all that God heals it all.
So keep your head high and walk tall.

GOD PEP TALK

Things seem hard right now, but you can't let the past get you down.
Right now you have to be strong.
Forget about what others think is wrong.
You made a change in your life.
You decided you wanted to do something right.
I know it's going to be hard sometimes, but I will be there every time.
Your shoulder to cry on, someone to talk to, I will make sure you make it through.
I have a lot of faith in you.

I know that many have passed you by and yes you have a right to cry.
But then you have to dry your eyes, be strong and know that you did your best.
Now is the time for you have passed the test.
Another chance is in the making, all you have to do is take it.
Please I'll guide you, try my best to show you the way.
Just don't give up, soon there will be even better days.

I knew you before your birth, I have helped you dry your tears.
I know all your fears.
Just so you know I am always here.
I've got faith in you and I'm going to see you through.
See you become a successful you.
You are my child and for that I love you unconditionally, regardless of your difficulties.
So please do your best to be obedient and keep faith in me.
Work hard and I promise I'll help you grow successfully.

GOOD FAITH

Good faith is fortune
But no one ever knows its treasures.
Ones that have no measure
And placed at priceless.
For God is not one to impress.
For no one is perfect nor to judge the different dialect.

Good faith is in honor.
The pride that seeps through like the blood coming from a donor.
Not yet found its owner.
Then to plea… to breathe

Good faith is hope.
Holding on to what is precious.
Yet allowing the lord to show you what is true and right.
Free the passion that thrives in thee.
Free the soul that needs to be…
Released

For good faith is you.
The utter in your stutter of nervousness.
Your shame in past selfishness.
But you look to move on.
Move on because your strong.
Stronger than you lead on to believe.
Stronger than you want some to see.
Stronger than you want to be.
But you have a light.
A fire that burns into souls.
A purpose and a goal.
And you have you.
For you need you to do the things I need you to do.
So please, Love yourself.
And always, always to yourself be true.

Yes Father … I will.
Amen